THE LITTLE BOOK OF OLIVE OIL TIPS

ANDREW LANG

THE LITTLE BOOK OF OLIVE OIL TIPS

ANDREW LANGLEY

Absolute Press

First published in Great Britain in 2008 by
Absolute Press
Scarborough House, 29 James Street West
Bath BA1 2BT, England
Phone 44 (0) 1225 316013 **Fax** 44 (0) 1225 445836
E-mail info@absolutepress.co.uk
Web www.absolutepress.co.uk

A catalogue record of this book is available from the British Library

ISBN 13: 9781904573913

Printed and bound in China by 1010

'...I like them all, but especially the olive.
For what it symbolizes, first of all –
peace with its leaves,
and joy with its golden oil.'

Aldous Huxley (1894-1963)

1

Always have olive oil on your table at mealtimes.

Think of it as another seasoning, like salt and black pepper. A little drop of oil adds something to most dishes – not just pasta and salads but soups, stews, grilled fish and roast meats.

2

Read the label on the bottle before you buy.

There's no standard formula, but you should at least make sure of a) where it comes from, b) how it was processed (cold-pressed, etc.) and c) what has gone into it (non-olive oils, olive oils from different sources). In general, the more information on the label, the better the oil.

3

Is it OK to cook with olive oil?

Frying or roasting with a very good olive oil is a bit of a waste, as the high temperatures will destroy its delicacy. Also, the sediment in unfiltered oil will char and create a burnt taste. Use cheaper blended and filtered oils instead.

4

Cold-pressed extra virgin is the top grade

of olive oil. This means it has been extracted from the olives by mechanical or other physical means, and without the use of heat. It will be low in acidity and high in character. Keep it for salads, cold sauces, dips and other dressings rather than for cooking.

5

Olive oil tasting #1: the colour.

Judging an oil is not all that different from tasting a wine. Pour some into a glass and hold it to the light. Most high-quality oils have a greeny-golden colour. This is both a delight to the eye and a sign of health-giving antioxidants such as beta-carotene.

6

Blended olive oil can be produced in many ways.

It may contain oils from different vintages and even different countries. A good part will be lower-quality oil extracted by metal rollers and grinders, which tend to heat the pulp. The heat encourages the oil to flow, but also affects the final flavour.

7

Always check the age of an oil if possible.

Oil, unlike wine, does not improve with age. The harvesting vintage should be marked on the label of highest-quality olive oil. Such oils should be used within two years of their harvest – if not much sooner. Otherwise, you'll have to rely on the 'best before' date on the bottle.

8

Olive oil **may go cloudy or even solid when refrigerated.**

Never fear: just leave it at room temperature for a while and it will resume its normal state without noticeable loss of flavour. Better still: keep it out of the fridge altogether – the chill will encourage condensation and rancidity.

9

Once a bottle of virgin oil is opened,

use it up within a couple of months.

That means only buying a bottle which will last you for that period. The delicate acids and fats will begin to deteriorate once exposed to the air. Blended and processed oils will last a little longer.

10

Olive oil tasting #2: the aroma.

If you're ever in an olive oil mill, find a big vat of the the stuff and sniff deeply – it's a glorious experience. Failing that, sniff some in a glass. The aroma of the best oils should contain hints of flowers, citrus or other fruit, and a touch of nuttiness and grassiness. No smell, no class.

11

Olive oil is very sensitive to light and heat.

Light damages the natural chlorophyll in the oil, leading to oxidation. Heat degrades the proteins. Both make the oil smell stale and taste rancid. So store your olive oil in a can or dark glass bottle, in a cool, dark place.

12

Keep two or three olive oils in stock.

For dressings, dips and drizzling on bread, have a nice green oil which is cold-pressed and extra virgin. Choose a lighter extra virgin for variety, and add a milder, cheaper oil for frying, grilling and roasting.

13

One of the

simplest and quickest pasta dishes features olive oil. While the pasta (spaghetti) is simmering, warm a generous glug of oil with chopped garlic and chilli. Add some chopped parsley. Toss this sauce with the cooked pasta.

14

The best way to serve vegetable soup:

with olive oil. Place a slice of bread in the bowl and pour on a generous slug of oil. Then ladle the soup on top. The heat releases the magical scents of the oil, while the oil adds something subtle to the soup's texture.

15

Olive oil tasting #3: the taste.

It may seem strange, but take a sip from the glass. Roll it round your mouth and over your tongue. Rate the oil for pepperiness and bitterness. If it lightly burns in your throat, that's often a sign of good quality. If you're tasting more than one oil, spit out rather than swallowing.

16

Roast potatoes in olive oil.

Put 1½kg (3lb) of quartered potatoes in a roasting dish and season with salt, pepper and oregano. Mix 3 tablespoons of olive oil with the juice of 2 lemons and pour over the potatoes, along with a slosh of water. Roast at high heat for 15 minutes, then lower for 30–45 minutes.

17

You can

use olive oil in place of butter

in many types of recipe, from baking to braising. Here's a rough conversion chart: for one tablespoon of butter, use $^3/_4$ tablespoon of oil, and for 225ml (8fl oz) butter, use 170ml (6 fl oz) oil.

18

Aioli is the quintessential olive oil and garlic sauce

– rich, delicious and irresistible. In a blender, mix crushed garlic with two egg yolks. Then add, with agonizing gradualness, 125ml ($^{1}/_{4}$ pint) of extra virgin oil and the juice of half a lemon. Season with salt and pepper.

19

Tasty **olive oil is an integral part of gazpacho,** the legendary Spanish soup. In a processor, blend 1kg (2lb) tomatoes, 3 cloves garlic, a chopped green pepper, $^{3}/_{4}$ of a peeled cucumber, a chopped onion and a good handful of breadcrumbs. Add 3 tablespoons of olive oil, 2 of wine vinegar, salt and pepper. Serve cold.

20

For Greek olive bread, froth up yeast in tepid water mixed with honey. Add 3 tablespoons of olive oil. Stir the mixture into 450g (1lb) of warmed wholemeal flour with 2 teaspoons of salt. Knead well and let rise for 2 hours. Mix in chopped black olives and sautéed onion. Let rise for 30 minutes, then bake for about 35 minutes.

21

What could go better together than olive oil and olives?

They are the basis of tapenade, that most Provençal of spreads. Whizz up some pitted black olives with slightly smaller quantities of capers and anchovies. Then slowly add as much olive oil as you like.

22

Spread your tapenade on croûtons.

Simply slice up a baguette (on the slant for aesthetic effect), dip the slices into a bowl of olive oil and bung them under the grill or in the oven for 10 minutes maximum.

23

Bagna cauda

(Italian for 'hot bath')

is a warm anchovy dip

made with plenty of olive oil. Lightly fry chopped garlic in 200ml (7fl oz) of oil with a knob of butter, then add 10 rinsed anchovies. Stir over a very low heat until it becomes smooth.
Dip in sliced celery, carrot, peppers and such.

24

Occasionally, a bottle of unrefined

olive oil may throw a dark deposit which will eventually spoil the flavour. It is easy to

filter this out.

Simply put some cotton wool into a funnel and pour the oil through it. Store the cleansed oil in a clean bottle.

25

Cheese and olive oil make a sumptuous, if surprising, **combination.**

Grate some Taleggio, Mozzarella or a mild and firmish goats cheese and pour on the oil. Leave, covered, in the fridge for a day. Serve at room temperature.

26

Lemons preserved in olive oil

add a new dimension to casseroles.

Soak 6 unsprayed lemons in several changes of water over 2 days. Slice thinly, discarding ends and pips, then sprinkle with salt. A day later, pack into glass jars with any brine residue, bay leaves and oregano. Cover with oil and leave for at least two weeks.

27

Skordalia mixes

olive oil with two other Greek staples – garlic and almonds. Whizz up 120g (4oz) of ground almonds with 4 cloves of garlic and seasoning. Then add – very slowly – 200ml (7fl oz) extra virgin oil plus 4 tablespoons of red wine vinegar. Serve with vegetable or chicken.

28

Try a **raw tomato and oil sauce with your pasta.** Chop and mash 450g (1lb) sweet tomatoes in a bowl. Add 120ml (4fl oz) olive oil, some chopped garlic and basil (or parsley), salt and pepper. Leave to develop its taste for 3 hours before mixing with cooked pasta.

29

The basic rule for **making flavoured olive oils** is: only **use dried ingredients.**

Fresh herbs, lemon peel or garlic all contain water, which may cause moulds and worse. So stick to dried herbs, fruit peels, chillis and so on.

30

For a good

spicy-flavoured olive oil, add 3 cinnamon sticks and 10 whole cloves to 500ml (16fl oz) of oil. Bottle and cork tightly, then leave to steep for at least 3 days.

31

Start the day with olive oil.

Try the traditional

Cretan breakfast

of virgin oil drizzled on good wholemeal bread and sprinkled with salt, pepper and fresh oregano. Much better than buttered toast.

32

Cooking globe artichokes? The easiest of all dips

to serve with this great vegetable consists of 5 parts extra virgin olive oil to 1 part freshly-squeezed lemon juice. A grinding of black pepper and a little salt add the final touches.

33

Hummous is another very simple dip,

in which **olive oil is essential.**

Drain and rinse a can of chickpeas, then whizz up with mashed garlic, 2 tablespoons tahini, lemon juice and seasoning. Add olive oil until it is a smooth paste. Taste and add more lemon or oil if necessary.

34

Olive oil and garlic paste goes beautifully **with roast meats.** Wrap 2 heads of garlic and a little oil in foil, and bake in a hot oven for about 30 minutes. Once it's cool, squeeze out the soft pulp and blend with enough oil (and a pinch of salt) to make a paste. Store in the fridge for up to 3 months.

35

Black olive and green lentil salad is a typical Greek dish which **demands good Greek olive oil.**

Boil 175g (6oz) lentils until soft. When cool, blend in a processor with a handful of pitted olives, 2 tablespoons capers, 2 anchovies, lemon juice, garlic and oregano. Add 4 tablespoons of olive oil slowly until creamy.

36

Olive oil plays a big role in paprika prawns.

Marinate uncooked prawns in a mixture of Spanish olive oil, crushed garlic, salt and hot smoked paprika for I hour. Then grill or griddle the prawns for 1 minute each side. Drain on paper towels and serve hot with lemon wedges.

37

A barbecued salad needs two doses of olive oil.

Thinly slice, salt and drain some aubergines and courgettes. Dry them, dip them in olive oil and grill on both sides. Then put them in a salad bowl, and add an olive oil and vinegar dressing, plus chopped parsley and toasted pine nuts.

38

A good salad dressing

(according to Italians), requires four people. A miser to put in the wine vinegar (1 part);

a spendthrift for the olive oil

(4 parts); a wise man for the salt (a pinch) and a lunatic to toss the salad (thoroughly). Very perceptive, Italians.

39

Olive oil is the **central element of a good marinade.**

The oil conditions and moistens meat and fish without drawing out the essential juices (which vinegar or wine tend to do). It also enhances the character of the herbs and other flavourings in the marinade.

40

Olive oil biscuits go perfectly with sweet wine.

Mix 270g (10oz) plain flour with 170g (6oz) brown sugar, ½ teaspoon baking soda, seasoning and chopped dried rosemary. Beat together 2 eggs, 110ml (4fl oz) olive oil and 170ml (6fl oz) red wine and combine with the dry ingredients. Bake as biscuits until light brown.

41

Bizarre but brilliant:

try olive oil on ice cream.

Put a couple of dollops of good vanilla ice cream in a bowl, then pour on a little tasty oil (preferably sweet and low in acidity). Add a small pinch of rock salt.

42

Olive oil makes a sumptuously moist apple cake. Beat together 150ml (5fl oz) oil, 200g (7oz) sugar and 2 eggs. Slowly add a mixture of 350g (12oz) flour, 2 teaspoons each of ground cinnamon and baking powder and a pinch of salt. Mix in 450g (1lb) chopped dessert apples, lemon zest and soaked sultanas. Bake for 1 hour.

43

Run out of shaving cream? Use olive oil

instead. It may seem a rather strange way to shave at first, but soon becomes very pleasurable. After all, it was good enough for the ancient Greeks and Romans.

44

Olive oil has **a miraculous effect on almost every part of the body.**

Put 3 tablespoons of it in your bath to condition your skin. Soak your nails for 10 minutes in a cup of it. Rub it on your feet before you go to bed. You can even rub it into your hair to get rid of dandruff and frizz.

45

Mix up your own **olive oil night cream.**

Blend two parts of a light oil with one part white wine vinegar and one part water. Lightly wet your face before applying this simple lotion.

46

This really does work. If you have an

ear bunged up with wax,

gently warm up a $\frac{1}{4}$ teaspoon of plain olive oil, tip your head and pour it in. After a few moments, tip your head the other way. Have a towel or tissues handy. The oil will soften and maybe even melt the offending wax.

47

Olive oil has a **cleansing and rejuvenating effect on wood.** Wipe it (sparingly) over wooden chopping boards and bowls, to prevent them drying out and cracking. You can also rub oil on dark wooden furniture. It **brings out the grain** and can get rid of water marks and other blemishes.

48

To remove olive oil stains

on clothing, cover the offending area with generous amounts of cornflour, salt or baking powder (though check first on the colour fastness). Leave for an hour, then scrape off. Wash the garment at a high temperature.

49

What is

pomace oil?

Pomace is the last gasp of the olive, extracted from the pressed remains, mostly by the use of solvents. It is then refined and blended with other oil. Pomace oil is the cheapest kind of olive oil you can buy.

Avoid it.

50

Many extravagant claims have been made for the **medicinal benefits of olive oil.** But there's no doubt it has amazing qualities. It is low in solid fats, high in vitamins A and E, and easy to digest. It helps us absorb calcium and resist hypertension and some cancers. It even acts as a painkiller.

Andrew Langley

Andrew Langley is a knowledgeable food and drink writer. Among his formative influences he lists a season picking grapes in Bordeaux, several years of raising sheep and chickens in Wiltshire and two decades drinking his grandmother's tea. He has written books on a number of Scottish and Irish whisky distilleries and is the editor of the highly regarded anthology of the writings of the legendary Victorian chef Alexis Soyer.

THE LITTLE BOOK OF
BARBECUE
TIPS
ANDREW LANGLEY

THE LITTLE BOOK OF
BEER
TIPS
ANDREW LANGLEY

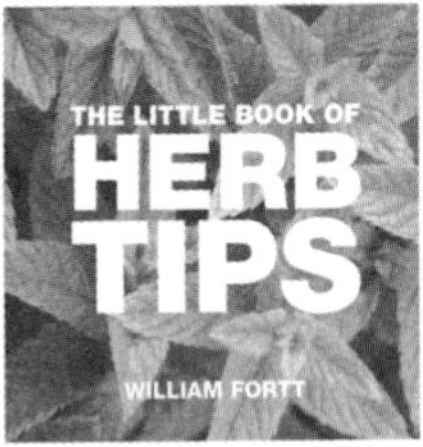
THE LITTLE BOOK OF
HERB
TIPS
WILLIAM FORTT

THE LITTLE BOOK OF
POKER
TIPS

THE LITTLE BOOK OF
GARDENING
TIPS
WILLIAM FORTT

THE LITTLE BOOK OF
CHEFS'
TIPS
RICHARD

THE LITTLE BOOK OF
SPICE
TIPS
ANDREW LANGLEY

THE LITTLE BOOK OF
GOLF
TIPS
PETER FRENCH

THE LITTLE BOOK OF
TIPS
SERIES

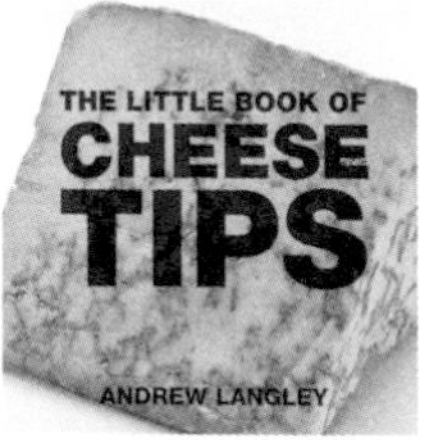
THE LITTLE BOOK OF
CHEESE
TIPS
ANDREW LANGLEY

THE LITTLE BOOK OF
WINE
TIPS
ANDREW LANGLEY

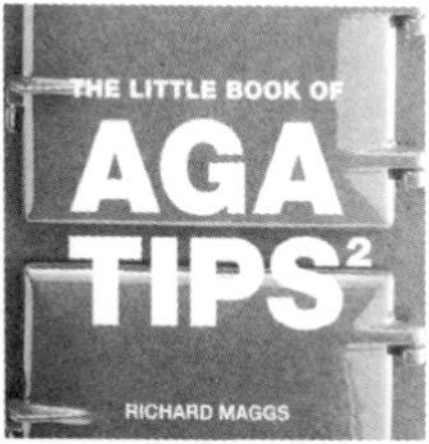
THE LITTLE BOOK OF
AGA
TIPS 2
RICHARD MAGGS

THE LITTLE BOOK OF
COFFEE
TIPS
ANDREW LANGLEY

THE LITTLE BOOK OF
TEA
TIPS
ANDREW LANGLEY

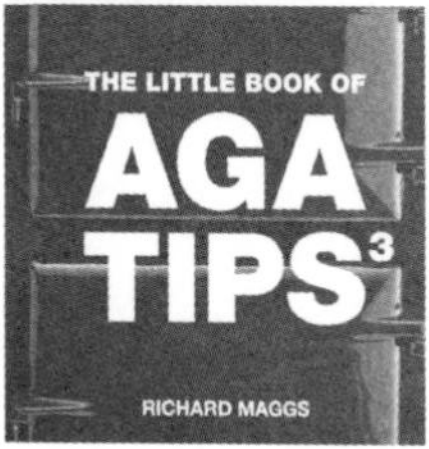
THE LITTLE BOOK OF
AGA
TIPS 3
RICHARD MAGGS

THE LITTLE BOOK OF
AGA
TIPS
RICHARD MAGGS

THE LITTLE BOOK OF
CHRISTMAS
AGA
TIPS
RICHARD MAGGS

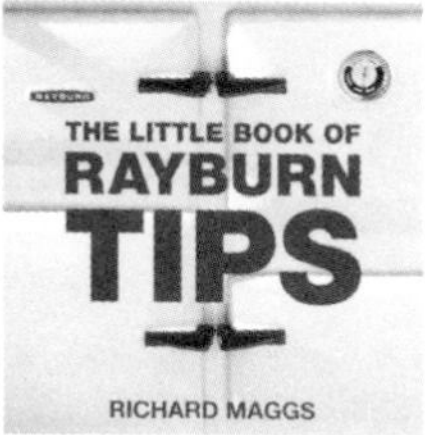
THE LITTLE BOOK OF
RAYBURN
TIPS
RICHARD MAGGS

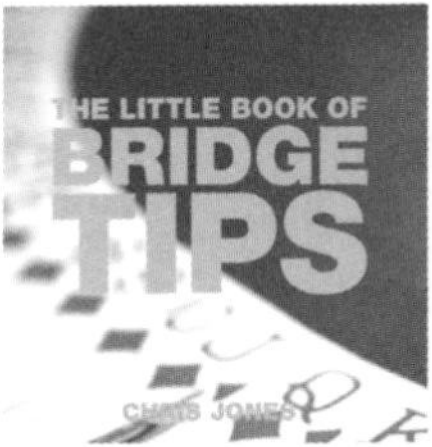
THE LITTLE BOOK OF
BRIDGE
TIPS

THE LITTLE BOOK OF
CHESS
TIPS
PETER FRENCH

THE LITTLE BOOK OF
FISHING
TIPS
MICK DEVENISH

THE LITTLE BOOK OF
GREEN
TIPS
WILLIAM FORTT

THE LITTLE BOOK OF
KITTEN
TIPS
ANDREW LANGLEY

MARMITE
THE LITTLE BOOK OF
MARMITE
TIPS

THE LITTLE BOOK OF
PUPPY
TIPS
ANDREW LANGLEY

THE LITTLE BOOK OF
WHISKY
TIPS
ANDREW LANGLEY

THE LITTLE BOOK OF
TRAVEL
TIPS
MEGAN DEVENISH

Little Books of Tips from Absolute Press

Aga Tips
Aga Tips 2
Aga Tips 3
Backgammon Tips
Barbecue Tips
Beer Tips
Bread Tips
Bridge Tips
Cake Decorating Tips
Cheese Tips
Chefs' Tips
Chess Tips
Christmas Aga Tips
Coffee Tips
Fishing Tips
Gardening Tips
Golf Tips
Green Tips
Hair Tips
Herb Tips
Houseplant Tips
Kitten Tips
Marmite Tips
Nail Tips
Olive Oil Tips
Poker Tips
Puppy Tips
Rayburn Tips
Scrabble Tips
Spice Tips
Tea Tips
Travel Tips
Vinegar Tips
Whisky Tips
Wine Tips

All titles: £2.99 / 112 pages